Boats and Ships

Angela Royston

Illustrated by
John Downes

Heinemann Interactive Library
Des Plaines, Illinois

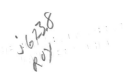

Contents

© 1998 Reed Educational & Professional Publishing
Published by Heinemann Interactive Library, an imprint of Reed Educational & Professional Publishing,
1350 East Touhy Avenue, Suite 240 West
Des Plaines, Illinois 60018

Library of Congress Cataloging-in-Publication Data
Royston, Angela.
    Boats and ships/Angela Royston; illustrated by John Downes.
        p. cm. — (Inside and out)
    Includes bibliographical references and index.
    Summary: Describes various kinds of water craft, including
tugboats, sailboats, and warships.
    ISBN 1-57572-170-8
    1. Boats and boating — Juvenile literature 2. Ships — Juvenile literature.
[1. Boats and boating. 2. Ships.] I. Downs, John, ill. II. Title. III. Series.
VM150.R69 1997   97-19339
623.8—dc21   CIP
                                                                      AC

Photo credits: page 7: © ZEFA; page 9, 14 and 21: © J. Allan Cash Ltd; page 11: © ZEFA-DEUTER;
page 12: FLPA © T Whittaker; page 13: Britstock-IFA © Eve Klein; page 19: Tony Stone Worldwide © David Higgs; page 22: © TRH/Royal Navy.

Editor: Alyson Jones; Designer: Peter Clayman; Picture Researcher: Liz Eddison
Art Director: Cathy Tincknell; Production Controller: Lorraine Stebbing

Printed and bound in Italy.
See-through pages printed by SMIC, France.

02 01 00 99 98
10 9 8 7 6 5 4 3 2 1

13.95

Boating for Fun

Boats carry people or things across water. Many people also sail boats just for fun. Can you see the speedboat pulling a waterskier? Windsurfers cut through the water, but they are not as fast as the speedboat!

A cabin cruiser is like a floating home. It has seats and bunk beds inside. Just right for a vacation on water!

The person inside this kayak is wearing a lifejacket and helmet in case it is tipped over by strong waves.

Carrying Cargo

Cargo ships carry things from place to place —even halfway around the world! Oil tankers are the biggest cargo ships. Underneath the long deck are huge tanks filled with oil. Ships and cars need oil to make them run.

These boats carry a different kind of cargo. They belong to farmers in Southeast Asia. The farmers paddle down the river to sell their vegetables.

At the Port

There is a lot to see in a port. A red tugboat is pulling a container ship into port. An orange crane is unloading large containers from a ship. Only one container fits onto a truck.

The harbor on the right shelters smaller boats. How many can you count in the harbor?

Look at all the boats
packed into this small
harbor in Greece.
It is so full the boats
have to tie up close
together.

9

Sailing Boats

In some parts of the world, sailing boats are still used for fishing or to carry cargo. People also sail boats for fun. The wind catches in the sails and blows the boat along. The stronger the wind blows, the faster the boat goes.

These sailboats are in a race. The crew lean far back to balance the sails. Can you see one person on each boat moving the rudder? This steers the boat. The other person hauls in the sails.

This Chinese sailing boat is called a junk. It is made of wood and has linen sails. Even though it looks old, it is a very strong, safe boat.

For hundreds of years, people have sailed across the oceans in boats like this. Sailors climb up the masts to take in the sails.

 # Ferries

Ferries sail at certain times each day or week. The biggest ferries carry cars, buses, and trucks, as well as people. A big door at the front of the ferry rises up and the vehicles drive on.

This ferry in Guyana carries goods and people. Can you see what was unloaded?

In India people cross from the island of Goa to the mainland on a small ferry. These people rush up the gangway to go to work.

Skimming the Waves

Hydrofoils and hovercraft are used to carry people from one island to another, across lakes, and even across the sea. As a hydrofoil moves forward, the wings underneath it push down on the water and raise the boat.

A hovercraft can travel over land as well as water. It moves on a cushion of air which is trapped beneath the hovercraft.

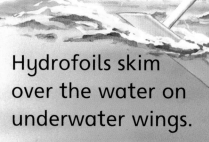

Hydrofoils skim over the water on underwater wings.

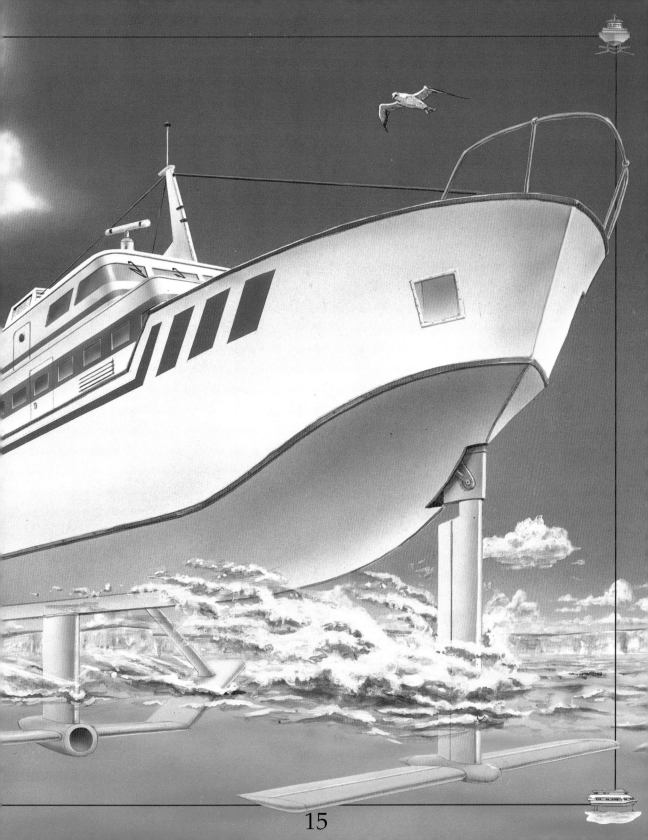

Fishing Boats

Some fishing boats carry nets that will be used to catch fish. One of these fishermen will use large pots which he will lower down to the seabed. He hopes that lobsters and crabs will scuttle into the pots!

This African fisherman throws a large net over the fish and pulls them in. The poles on the other side of the canoe stop it from tipping over.

Bigger fishing boats can stay at sea for several weeks. The biggest boats have huge freezers on board to keep the fish fresh.

Soon the crew of the fishing boat will pull in their net full of fish. Who else is hoping to catch a fish today?

17

# Under the Sea

Small submarines are called submersibles. They travel thousands of feet into the depths of the sea. Submersibles are used to inspect and mend pipes and cables under the sea. Others are used to explore shipwrecks or the seabed.

This submersible does not have people inside. It uses video cameras to send pictures back to a ship on the surface.

Can you see the diver? She is getting ready to explore outside this submersible.

The biggest submarines are warships. They can stay underwater for months at a time, but they can also sail on the surface.

Cruising Ships

Cruise ships are like floating hotels. Passengers sleep in cabins and spend their vacations sailing from place to place across the seas. There are plenty of things to do on board. Can you see the swimming pools on the deck?

Large lifeboats hang at the sides of the cruise ship.

Paddleboats used to carry cargo and passengers up and down the Mississippi river in the United States. This one now carries tourists.

This small cruise boat takes tourists on a tour of the canals of Amsterdam, Holland. Lots of other boats travel on these canals.

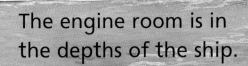

The engine room is in the depths of the ship.

Warships

The biggest warships are aircraft carriers. They are floating airports for military planes. The planes can land and refuel on the aircraft carrier and then return to duty.

This destroyer can fire guided missiles to protect submarines and aircraft. A computer guides the missile to its target.

Pilots need a lot of skill
to make their planes
take off and land on the
moving deck. They must
not miss the runway!

Glossary

Cabin Small room in a ship.
Container Large box in which cargo (goods) is stored.
Crew Team of people who work together on a boat.
Deck Platform or top surface of a ship.
Freezers Machine that keeps things inside it cold.
Gangway Opening by which a ship is boarded.
Lifejacket Special vest made of material that makes you float in water
Mast Long pole from which the ship's sails hang.
Paddleboat Boat that moves when a wheel is powered by steam.
Rudder Object fixed to the back of a boat which is used to steer it.
Windsurfer Someone who moves across the water on a board with a sail.

More Books To Read

Otfinoski, Steven. *Into the Wind: Sailboats Then and Now.* Tarrytown, NY: Benchmark, 1997.
Gibbons, Gail. *Boat Book.* New York: Holiday House, 1983.
Crews, Donald. *Harbor.* New York: Mulberry Books, 1982.

Index